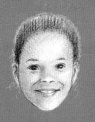

DK

A DK PUBLISHING BOOK

Editor Nicola Waine
Designer Emma Bowden
Design Assistance Diane Clouting
Managing Editor Linda Martin
Managing Art Editor Julia Harris
US Editor Camela Decaire
Editorial Consultant David Gillingwater
DTP Designer Nicky Studdart
Production Lisa Moss

First American Edition,1997
2 4 6 8 10 9 7 5 3 1
Published in the United States by DK Publishing, Inc.
95 Madison Avenue, New York, New York 10016

DK would like to thank
Barnabas and Anabel Kindersley for the use of their
photographs, previously published in
Children Just Like Me.

Published in Great Britain by
Dorling Kindersley Ltd.
A catalog record for this book is available from the
Library of Congress

ISBN 0-7894-1502-X

Color reproduction by GRB, Italy
Printed in Belgium by Proost.

You·Can·Draw
AMAZING FACES
Kim Gamble

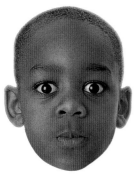

Contents

6 Shapes and lines

8 Drawing features

10 Expressions

12 Family features

13 Caricatures

14 Hair, hats, and glasses

16 Light and shade

17 Techniques and materials

18 Profiles

19 Three-quarter views

20 Different angles

21 Adding character

DK PUBLISHING, INC.

Shapes and lines

Drawing a face is not as hard as you might think. The basic shape of all faces is an egg – round at the top and narrower at the bottom. Features such as the eyes, nose, ears, and mouth are nearly always made from simple circles and curves. Once you can see these shapes on a face, you are ready to begin drawing.

The eyes are halfway between the top of the head and the chin, and level with the top of the ears.

The nose is usually about as wide as the space between the eyes.

Ears are simple curves on the sides of the head. They begin level with the eyes and end at the bottom of the nose.

The mouth is about a third of the distance from the nose to the tip of the chin. The corners should be aligned with the centers of the eyes.

Look for details
Although most faces can be drawn by following the same rules, each one has slightly different features. It is these details that make us all look individual.

Hair changes the shape of the head.

Eyebrows can be curved or straight.

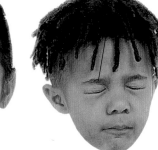

Remember that mouths can be smiling, sad, open, or closed.

Notice the shape of the eyes.

Look for lines between the nose and the mouth.

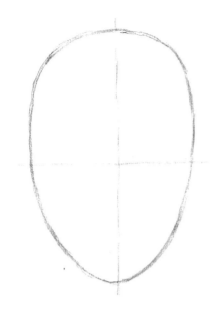

1 First draw an egg shape. Divide it into quarters through the center with light pencil lines. This will help you place the eyes, nose, and mouth on the face.

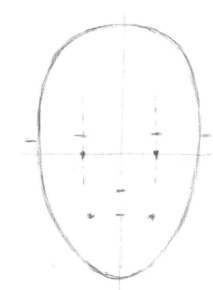

2 Draw faint points on the face to show where the main features will be. The eyes should be about halfway down the face, along the horizontal guideline.

3 Draw in the main features. The eyes are ovals, and the mouth has a curved bottom lip and a straight top lip. The hairline is a curve from ear to ear across the forehead.

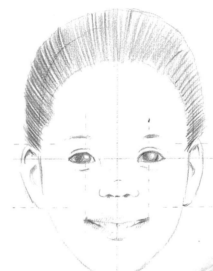

4 Add detail to the eyes and mouth. Draw the nose by making a faint circle, then add the curves of the nostrils on each side. Start to fill in the hair with soft strokes.

5 Draw lines from the nostrils to the corners of the mouth to show the cheeks. When you are happy with your drawing, erase the guidelines and add detail to the hair and the ears.

6 To make your picture look three dimensional, add some shading. Make your main lines darker, then shade the face with colored pencils, paints, chalk pastels, or crayons (see pp.14-15).

Drawing features

Now that you have learned where to place the main features on the guidelines, you can concentrate on detail and accuracy. The positioning rules apply to all faces, but remember that individual features on each face are different.

Drawing eyes

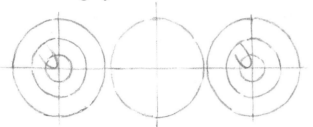

1 The distance between the eyes is roughly equal to the width of one of the eyes. Add inner circles for the iris and pupil.

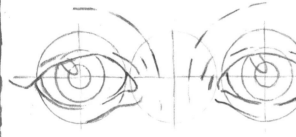

2 Draw the basic oval eye shapes. The outline of the eye sockets breaks the middle circle into thirds.

3 Shade the eye sockets for depth. Add a few strokes for the eyelashes and color the irises, leaving a glint of light.

From the side

An eyeball is a circle, and the iris and pupil are ovals. The eyelids form a triangle from the center point of the guidelines.

Notice that the face is slightly angled to the left.

8

Ears and nose

Like all of the features on a face, the ears and nose are drawn from basic shapes. The ear is two half ovals and the nose is a circle and two triangles.

Very short hair emphasizes the shape of the head.

1 The basic oval shapes are positioned on the side of the face.

2 Position the inside curve to follow the shape of the upper oval.

3 Add shading to show that the inside curve is the hollow of the ear.

1 Draw a circle for the tip of the nose and an elongated triangle for the main part.

2 Add the nostril curves. Draw the bridge of the nose where the triangles overlap.

3 Shade around the bridge, the nostrils, and the tip for depth.

Drawing a mouth

Mouths can be many different shapes depending on the mood of the person you are drawing. Notice whether the teeth are showing and how full the lips are.

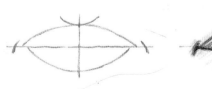

1 To draw a closed mouth, start with two guidelines and a simple oval shape. Add the indent at the top.

2 Draw the outline of the mouth, then shade. Now try drawing the other mouths shown here.

A wide smile like this creates dimples.

Expressions

The shapes and lines on our faces not only make us look different, they also reveal the way we are feeling. Look carefully at a face before you begin to draw it to see if you can tell what mood the person is in from their expression.

Looking for clues
Study the expression on this face. Features change with each different mood and will give you clues about how a person is feeling. This happy face has wide eyes and a broad smile.

1 Start your drawing in the usual way, with a basic shape and guidelines to help you position the features.

2 Draw the points for the main features on the face. Then you can begin to think about the expression.

3 Lightly draw the line of the mouth, the eyebrows, and the shape of the eyes on your face shape.

4 Draw the mouth with a gently curving smile. Add lines between the cheeks and nose.

5 Add the ears and detail to the eyes. Include the small lines around the eyes where the cheeks are lifting.

6 Finally, add the hair and fill in the details. Emphasize the eyes and mouth to create a rounded, smiling face.

A smile lifts the cheeks, which makes the eyes narrower.

When a face expresses anger, the eyes point down and the nostrils are flared.

A face looks open and rounded when expressing happiness.

The eyes and mouth turn down when a face expresses sadness.

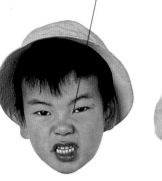
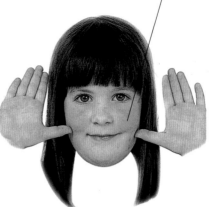

Smiling
When the mouth is smiling, it creates gentle curves in the cheeks and lifts the face to make it appear more rounded.

Angry
Eyebrows tell us a lot about a person's mood. When they are pointing down toward the nose, the face looks angry.

Happy
You can quickly tell what mood a person is in by looking at their eyes. Bright, rounded eyes like this are found on a happy face.

Sad
A sad face without a smile to lift the cheeks is often longer than a happy one. The mouth turns down and the eyes are small.

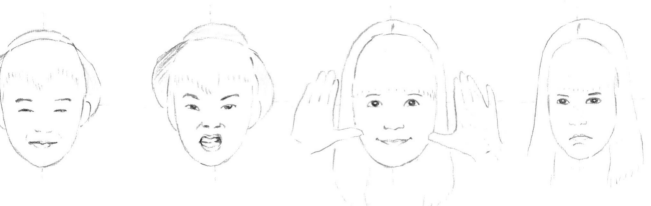

Recognizing the expression
Look at the photographs and try to draw their expressions using the illustrations above as guides. Then try to match the following moods with the expressions on the faces below; surprised, happy, afraid, wicked, sad. Draw your own faces with different expressions, then add colors that you think reflect the moods.

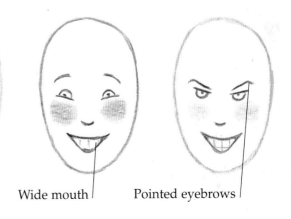

Narrow eyes   Wide eyes   Downturned mouth   Wide mouth   Pointed eyebrows

Family features

The members of this family look different. But look closely – they all have similar features. Try drawing them by following the illustrated steps.

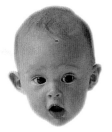

Baby
Babies' foreheads look proportionally bigger than adults'. Use a soft pencil for the features.

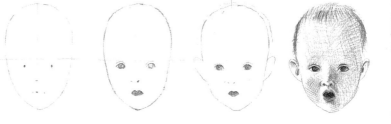

Sister
She has a rounded chin like her mother's, with full, high cheeks and narrow lips.

Brother
His ears and chin are similar to his baby brother's. His cheeks are thinner than his sister's.

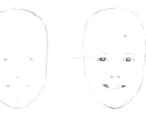

Mother
She has faint eyebrows and her lips are fuller than her daughter's. She has a high hairline.

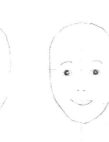

Father
He has a strongly shaped chin and jawbone and lips the same shape as his son's.

Grandparents
Now try drawing the grandparents on your own. Look for family likenesses to help you.

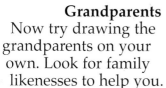

His forehead is the same squared shape as the father's.

His nose is very different from the rest of the family.

Caricatures

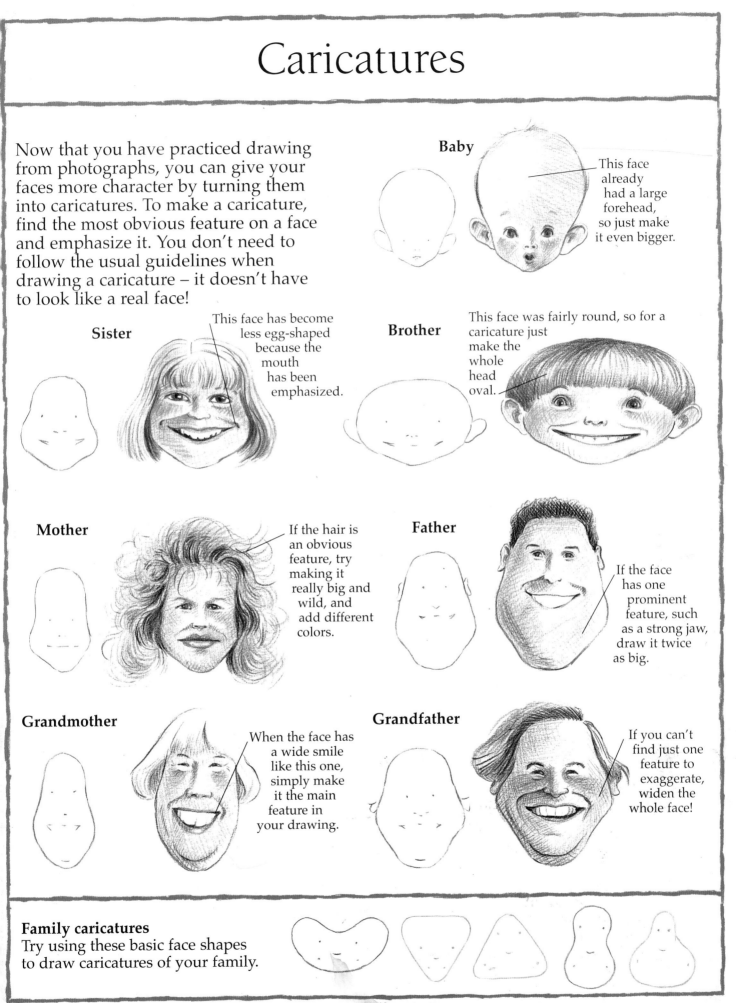

Now that you have practiced drawing from photographs, you can give your faces more character by turning them into caricatures. To make a caricature, find the most obvious feature on a face and emphasize it. You don't need to follow the usual guidelines when drawing a caricature – it doesn't have to look like a real face!

Baby

This face already had a large forehead, so just make it even bigger.

Sister

This face has become less egg-shaped because the mouth has been emphasized.

Brother

This face was fairly round, so for a caricature just make the whole head oval.

Mother

If the hair is an obvious feature, try making it really big and wild, and add different colors.

Father

If the face has one prominent feature, such as a strong jaw, draw it twice as big.

Grandmother

When the face has a wide smile like this one, simply make it the main feature in your drawing.

Grandfather

If you can't find just one feature to exaggerate, widen the whole face!

Family caricatures
Try using these basic face shapes to draw caricatures of your family.

Hair, hats, and glasses

Even straight hair is higher than the face shape.

When drawing a face with hair, a hat, or glasses, make the basic shapes before adding the accessories. Use the features as position guides.

Straight hair
Position the hair carefully. On this face the hair hangs over one of the eyes and ends above the chin.

Curly hair
No matter how short, long, or wild the hair is, it can be drawn from a simple shape. Don't try to draw each single hair, just add a few strokes for detail.

This basic hair shape is oval.

The ears show through the hair.

Wearing glasses
Draw the face and features first. To add the glasses, draw a lens centered over each eye, then join them together over the nose. Position the arms over the ears.

The hat sits where the hairline would be.

Straw hat
The top of a hat is a curve that sits higher than the basic egg shape, and a brim is two ovals. The smaller oval should cross the forehead where the hairline would be. The ovals are like rings around a planet.

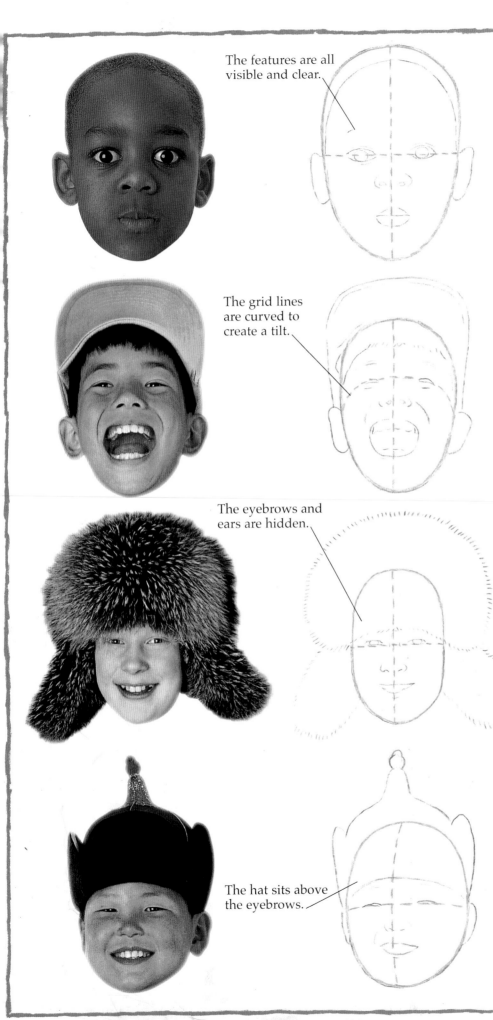

Bare head
When a face has very little hair, you can see the shape of the head clearly. But there is still a hairline curving from ear to ear. Try shading around the top of the forehead lightly to soften the hairline.

The features are all visible and clear.

Baseball cap
The whole hat may not always be visible. You can only see this hat from the underneath, so it looks simple. Draw a rectangle, then round off the corners. This face is tilted (see p.18), so you can see the nostrils.

The grid lines are curved to create a tilt.

Furry hat
This hat is about as high as the face is long, and is a simple shape. Draw the hat after you have positioned the features. The eyebrows do not show, but the eyes are smiling because the cheeks are lifting.

The eyebrows and ears are hidden.

Warrior hat
Draw this hat slightly taller than the head shape and add the spire on top. The head is turning to the left, so the guidelines have moved slightly (see p.17). Use them to help you form the shape of the hat.

The hat sits above the eyebrows.

15

Light and shade

You can create all the features of a face with shapes and lines, but it is light and shade that bring a face to life. Always look for three areas of color in a face: light, mid-tone, and dark.

Cross-hatching
This is a technique using light strokes in different directions to add shade to an area.

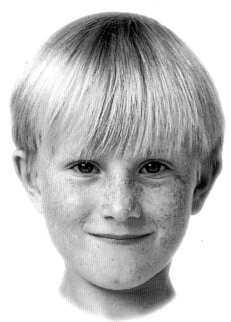

Shading a face
The light is coming from the left, casting shadows to the right.

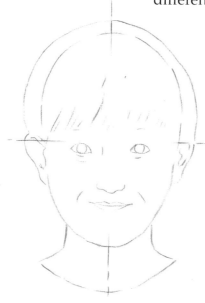

1 Using a pencil, lightly draw the basic shapes of the face, including the main features.

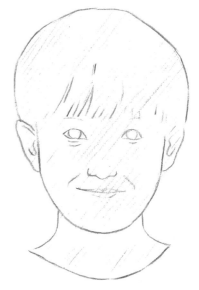

2 To create the first layer of shading, color across the face and hair with light brown.

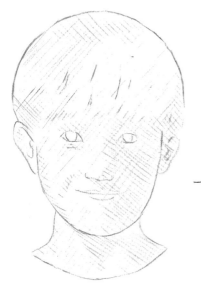

3 Now crosshatch lightly across the face, leaving the very light areas, as above.

4 Change to a red-brown color and crosshatch in the mid-tone areas to define them.

5 Crosshatch again for the darker areas, and finish with dark brown for the deep shades.

Materials and techniques

Whichever materials you are using to color and shade, it always helps to draw your subject lightly in pencil first. You can then either erase or color over the guidelines.

Watercolor
Draw the face with faint pencil lines as usual. Start your painting with a pale yellow base.

Keep the paint even on the face. Add a second layer to show the darker, mid-tone shades.

Darken the face and hair by adding more layers over the base colors once each previous layer is dry.

Felt-tip pens
Leave areas of white between your strokes as you color – solid felt-tip pen can look too dark.

Keep the eyes white at first, and try to keep the direction of the strokes the same across the face and hair.

Using a darker brown, add detail to the hair and the main features on top of the shading.

Crayons
Using the broad end of the crayon, color the whole face and hair in a yellow-brown.

Begin to add shade and detail with a darker brown. Keep the crayon lines clear and broad.

With the thinner edge of the crayon, add detail and the dark shades to the features and the hair.

Chalk pastels
Put a layer of brown and yellow in the center of the face and rub it around with your finger.

Add the red-brown chalk and rub it into the first layer of color, spreading it evenly in the mid-tone areas.

Shade the dark tones with black, and use white chalk or an eraser to add light around the hair and nose.

Profiles

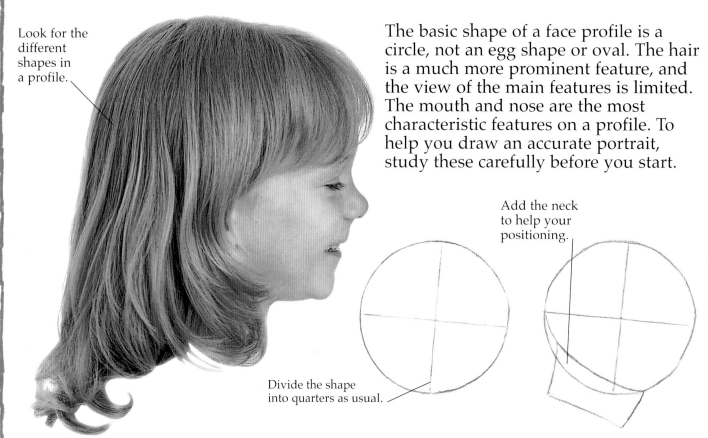

Look for the different shapes in a profile.

The basic shape of a face profile is a circle, not an egg shape or oval. The hair is a much more prominent feature, and the view of the main features is limited. The mouth and nose are the most characteristic features on a profile. To help you draw an accurate portrait, study these carefully before you start.

Add the neck to help your positioning.

Divide the shape into quarters as usual.

Circle practice
Drawing a clear circle takes practice. Keep your wrist loose and draw lightly until you are confident and accurate.

1 Draw the guidelines as above onto the circle. The horizontal line falls in the usual position.

2 Trim off the base of the circle as you draw the neck. This is a guideline for the jaw.

The hair sits above the head.

Start adding detail to the hair.

Gradually color over the guidelines.

3 Add the outline of the hair and the chin. The eye sits on the horizontal guideline.

4 Draw the nose as a curve outward and the mouth as a break in the face outline.

5 Add detail to the mouth and eyes. Finally, shade to make the head look rounded.

Three-quarter views

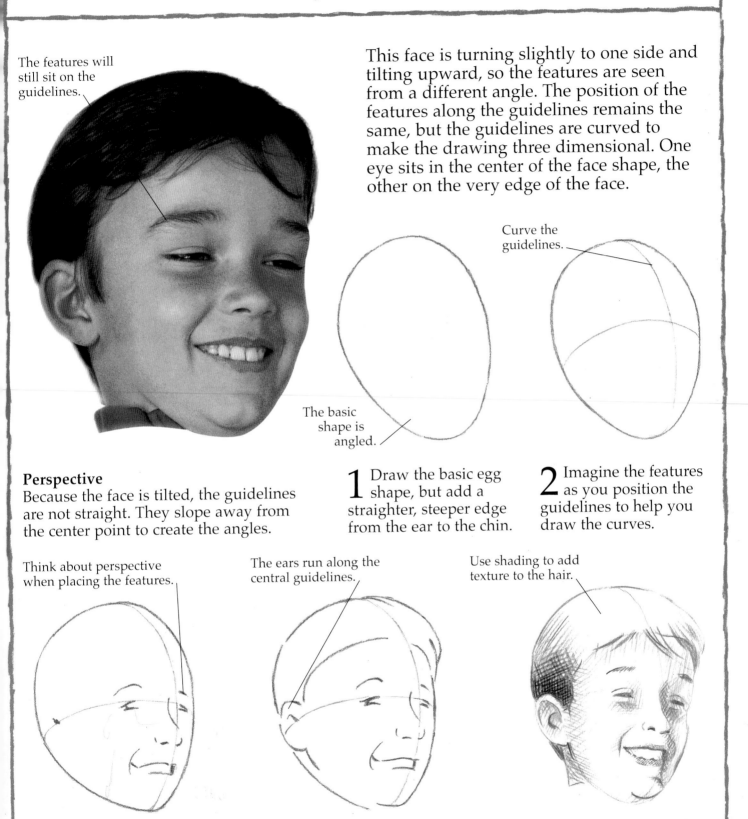

The features will still sit on the guidelines.

This face is turning slightly to one side and tilting upward, so the features are seen from a different angle. The position of the features along the guidelines remains the same, but the guidelines are curved to make the drawing three dimensional. One eye sits in the center of the face shape, the other on the very edge of the face.

Curve the guidelines.

The basic shape is angled.

Perspective
Because the face is tilted, the guidelines are not straight. They slope away from the center point to create the angles.

1 Draw the basic egg shape, but add a straighter, steeper edge from the ear to the chin.

2 Imagine the features as you position the guidelines to help you draw the curves.

Think about perspective when placing the features.

The ears run along the central guidelines.

Use shading to add texture to the hair.

3 Keep the features in place on the guidelines. Notice how the shapes have changed.

4 Draw the hairline onto the face. One of the ears can be seen clearly from this angle.

5 Add detail to the face and use color and shading to add depth to the angles.

Different angles

In order to draw a face from the top, bottom, or side, you need to know how to make an image look three dimensional. As a face turns, its features will change shape, depending on which angle you can see. The first rule when drawing a face from an angle is to curve the guidelines, as shown here. This will keep your points in position, and help you place the main features.

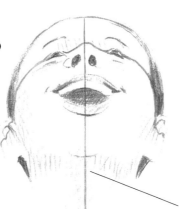

View from underneath
When the head is looking upward, you can see less of the forehead and more of the neck. The chin no longer forms the bottom of the face shape, and the nostrils are almost aligned with the eyes.

The chin is less defined from this angle, but the neck seems longer.

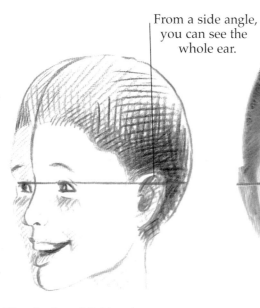

From a side angle, you can see the whole ear.

From the front, a face looks roughly symmetrical.

The back of the head looks round.

Vertical guideline
Turn the head sideways, and you can see dips and bumps appear along the vertical guideline. The line goes in at eye level, out for the nose, in again for the mouth, and finally out for the chin.

Crosshatching will make the top of the head look round.

This view makes the main features look closer together.

Different shapes
Look for the new shapes on a face when the head is turned sideways. An eye that appears oval from the front view may look more like a triangle from the side.

View from above
You can see more of the top of the head and the ears are a different shape. The eyes, nose, and mouth appear to have moved closer together along the vertical center guideline.

Adding character

Boys' faces

Once you have learned the basics, practice drawing this boy's face. Tilt the egg shape to 45° and add the guidelines, as shown. With all the features in place, you can start to create different characters.

This head is tilted back and has a laughing, open face.

Add the guidelines and position the features along them.

Fill in the detail and add shading to emphasize angle.

Make the hair white, and add a beard for a laughing old man.

Raise the eyebrows and open the eyes wide to imply fear.

To suggest stubble, lightly crosshatch in blue on the chin.

A new hat and a winking eye creates a different character.

Girls' faces

Now practice drawing this girl's face. Study it carefully and pick out the expression in the features. By changing the expression and adding accessories, you can create more new characters.

This girl's head is tilted to the side and she is winking.

Draw the guidelines and add the features, keeping one eye closed.

Fill in the detail and add color to bring the face to life.

Angled eyebrows and a crooked mouth can create a sinister look.

Add gray hair and glasses for an older woman.

Draw raised eyebrows and wide eyes for a surprised look.

Add accessories to create different fashion styles.

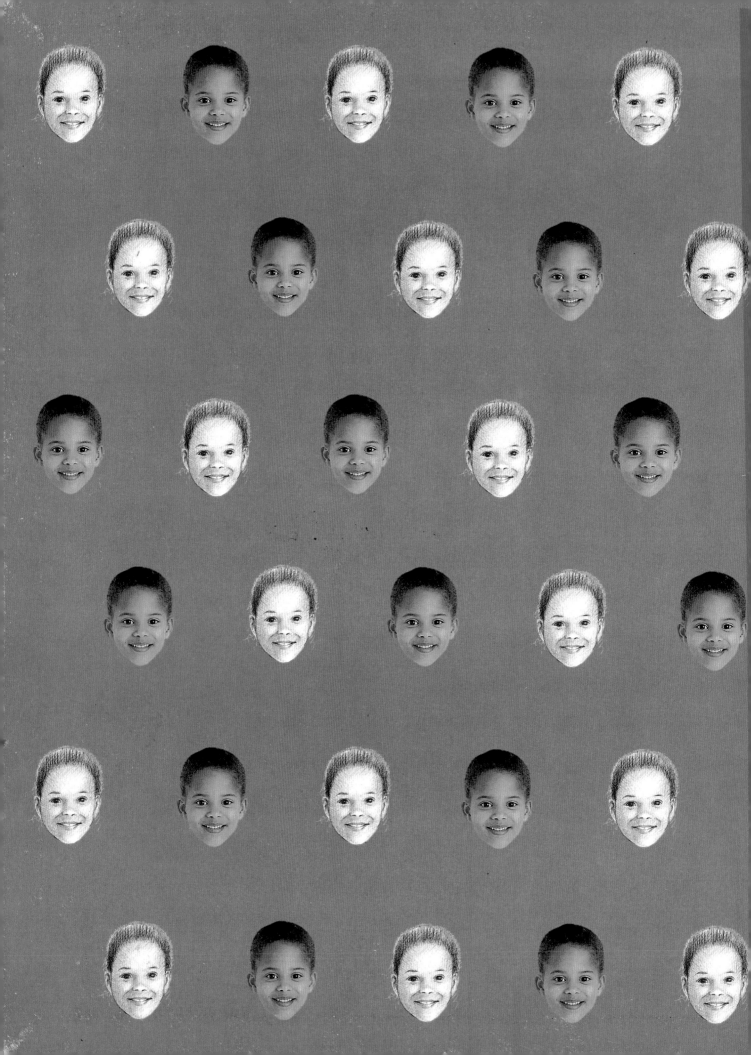